MOMMY, MOMMY,

I MISS you FROM WORK

AuthorHouse™
1663 Liberty Drive
Bloomington, IN 47403
www.authorhouse.com
Phone: 1 (800) 839-8640

Published by AuthorHouse 11/28/2018

ISBN: 978-1-5462-3821-8 (sc)
ISBN: 978-1-5462-3822-5 (e)
ISBN: 978-1-5462-3823-2 (hc)

Print information available on the last page.

This book is printed on acid-free paper.

authorHOUSE®

MOMMY, MOMMY,

I MISS YOU FROM WORK

KP DANIEL

Growing up as a small child l have fond memories of my mom.

Her soft curly hair, her beautiful smile, and the twinkle in her eyes.

As she whispered sweet words of encouragement to me....always telling me you can be anything you want to be... because you and your brother are my very special guys.

Always work hard, never give up, and always put God first.

It was these words that brought a sense of peace and confidence that I could tackle anything that came my way.

Her words I would remember and repeat throughout my life... that kept me going even on the toughest day.

My response was always the same... A simple phrase we shared throughout the years.

"Mom.... hold me tight and don't let go until the sun rises."

She would chuckle gently holding me tight as she kissed me goodnight, saying, "close your eyes my angel.. never forget mommy loves you... sleep tight"

It was this simple ritual that left me knowing everything was always alright.

When I woke in the morning it was to a gentle nudge and a warm touch on my bed...

saying ever so sweetly. Baby it's time to get up... wake up..wake up. Wake up you sleepy head.

My eyes would open and I would see her sweet face.

A gentle smile and tender glow, always followed by a warm embrace... for she was my saving grace.

It was these moments I'll never forget... the ones that burn deep in my soul.

For my mom was my everything, my constant, my rock, the one that made me whole.

She would tell me to get dressed and to be good in school...

remember you're there to learn... not act like a fool.

As she opened the front door to leave for work, I would reach up and put my arms around her waist, giving her a big hug from behind….whispering

Mommy…Mommy…I miss you from work. Why do you have to go?

Mommy…Mommy…I miss you from work. Tell me you love me so.

Always in a rush to head out the door, my mom would take the time and turn around to give me a big kiss and say.

"Don't worry, don't fret, I'll be home before the sun sets."

After school, I would come home, do my homework and await for her arrival.

Just like clockwork she would come thru the door like a preacher at a revival.

Beaming with light….her arms wide open, making everything in my day suddenly alright.

It would be this way for years to come.. having her by my side.. teaching, guiding, nurturing and sometimes scolding me... but always my gift from heaven.

I'm proud to say as I look back on those years,

Mommy….Mommy… I'm glad you went to work….you made me the person I am today.

Mommy... mommy... I'm glad you went to work... and made the sacrifices you made each day.

Mommy... mommy... I'm glad you went to work. You inspired me more than you'll ever know.

Mommy...Mommy... I'm glad you went to work...for it was your love and faith that helped me grow.

Printed in the United States
By Bookmasters